OXFORD

WILD READS

D1643057

Bees

Robert Dawson

OXFORD

UNIVERSITY PRESS

This book belongs to:

OXFORD
UNIVERSITY PRESS

Great Clarendon Street, Oxford OX2 6DP
Oxford University Press is a department of the University of Oxford.
It furthers the University's objective of excellence in research, scholarship,
and education by publishing worldwide in

Oxford   New York

Auckland   Cape Town   Dar es Salaam   Hong Kong   Karachi
Kuala Lumpur   Madrid   Melbourne   Mexico City   Nairobi
New Delhi   Shanghai   Taipei   Toronto

With offices in

Argentina   Austria   Brazil   Chile   Czech Republic   France   Greece
Guatemala   Hungary   Italy   Japan   Poland   Portugal   Singapore
South Korea   Switzerland   Thailand   Turkey   Ukraine   Vietnam

Oxford is a registered trade mark of Oxford University Press
in the UK and in certain other countries

Text © Robert Dawson
Illustrations © Steve Roberts
The moral rights of the author have been asserted

Database right Oxford University Press (maker)

This edition 2009

British Library Cataloguing in Publication Data

Data available

ISBN: 978-0-19-911924-0

1 3 5 7 9 10 8 6 4 2

Printed in China
Paper used in the production of this book is a natural,
recyclable product made from wood grown in sustainable forests.
The manufacturing process conforms to the environmental
regulations of the country of origin.

Contents

▶ Welcome to the city of bees   4

▶ Who lives in the city of bees?   6

▷ The landing and take-off area   9

▶ The streets   12

▶ The dance of the bees   16

▶ The wax factory   18

▶ The royal family   20

▷ The princess's story   24

▶ Bees, bumble-bees and wasps   28

▶ Glossary   30

▶ Welcome to the city of bees

The 60,000 bees living in this city are honey bees.

beehive

Honey bees are just one kind of bee.
There are many other kinds of bees
like cuckoo bees, mining bees and
leaf cutter bees.

honey bee

mining bee

cuckoo bee

leaf cutter bee

Who lives in the city of bees?

Many sorts of bees live in this city.

There are guards, messengers, factory workers, a queen with ladies-in-waiting, princes and princesses.

queen bee

There are baby bees, female bees
and a few male bees called drones.

All honey bees have special jobs to
do. They work hard in order to bring
food from flowers into their city and
turn the food into honey.

Here is a honey bee.

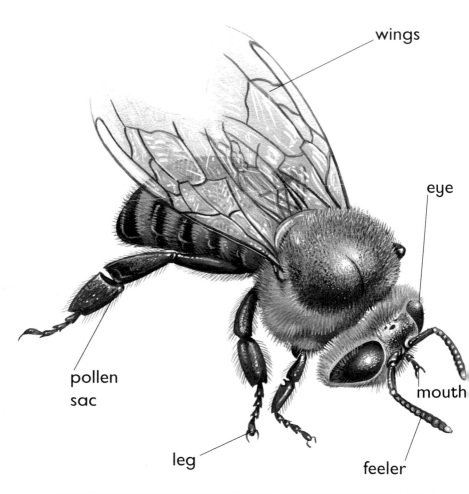

wings

eye

pollen
sac

mouth

leg

feeler

Did you know...
Bees don't breathe like people. They
have openings in their bodies through
which air passes.

The landing and take-off area

This city has a platform like an airport runway. Bees use this to come into the city with news of flowers ready for visiting, or to bring food.

A bee has just landed. She enters through the only gate. Like every other bee living in the city, she has a smell. The smell is special for that city. It's like a pass. Guards let bees with passes in. Others are attacked.

This bee is checked and let into the city. She passes some other guards who are flapping their wings. Their job all day and every day is to use their wings like fans to pull fresh air into the city.

▶ The streets

The bee is now inside the city.

The streets are made of huge combs of wax which hang down. The combs are made of beeswax and are very heavy.

Each comb has thousands of pot-like cells, each with six sides. The walls of each cell are thinner than tissue paper. Yet they are very strong.

Between each comb there is just enough room to allow two bees to work back to back.

There are thousands of worker bees buzzing to and fro and all of them are female.

The bee has come back after visiting a flower. She has a full basket on each leg, packed with either pollen or nectar. She unloads the pollen and nectar into cells. Some pollen is used to feed baby bees.

Now, other workers will make the nectar into honey to store for food in the winter.

collecting
pollen

unloading pollen

Did you know...
Pollen is like a dust in flowers? Some pollen gets stuck on the bee's hairs and is spread to another flower. This helps the flower grow seeds.

Did you know...
Nectar is a sweet liquid? It attracts bees to flowers. They take it back to their hives to make honey.

15

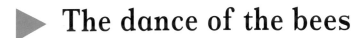

The dance of the bees

This bee found some nectar in a flowering currant bush a long way away. Now she has unloaded, she begins to dance and quiver. Her wings make a humming noise and waft the smell of the nectar about.

Other bees rush towards her. They examine the new nectar and all get very excited.

The way the bee dances and waggles her body tells the others how far away the food is, and in which direction to fly.

A group of bees sets off to find the new site of nectar. As they return, they dance and more and more bees rush to the new source of food.

Messenger bees, like this one, hold a very important job in the city.

making wax

► The wax factory

Wax is made in a special part of the hive. Wax is needed to build the combs. Only a few bees are allowed in here because it is very dangerous. Even the queen is banned.

The wax factory workers are very strong and well-fed bees. They crawl over and over each other in a ball shape. They get hotter and hotter. Wax sweats from them. It takes so much strength, each factory worker lives only a few days.

As more and more wax is made, the wax factory workers take it to different parts of the city. Here, others show them how and where to build new combs.

building cells
of a comb

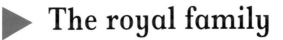

▶ The royal family

In the middle of the city, where it is safest, lives the queen. The queen is the leader of the city. Her guards have orders to attack anyone who disturbs her.

She has many bees to take care of her. She even has her own doctors who fetch special medicines from plants when she is ill.

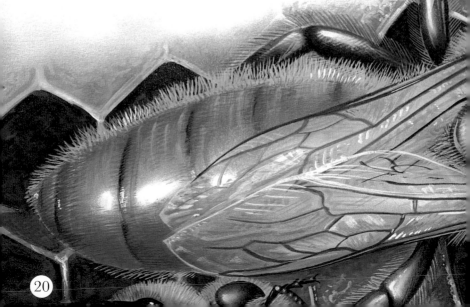

But her life is not easy. All the time her job is to lay eggs. This job is so important that she does not have time to stop to eat or clean herself. Instead, servants bring food and put it into her mouth. Others clean her with their feelers.

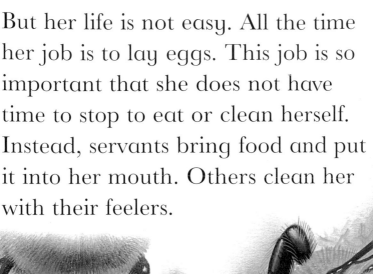

The queen is much bigger than the rest of the bees. All around her are lots of wax cells to hold babies. The queen lays an egg in one cell and goes on to the next.

When an egg hatches, nurse bees feed it. Then the nurses put a wax lid on the cell.

When it grows into a young bee, it chews through the lid of the cell to escape. Then it is given a job somewhere in the city.

the princess's cell

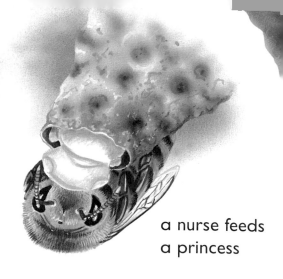

a nurse feeds a princess

The princess's story

But some baby bees are treated in a different way.

They are fed with Royal Jelly, a special food. They do not become workers in the city but grow into princesses and princes.

When the first princess appears, she immediately rips the wax lids off all her princess sisters' cells and kills them all. She is now the only princess.

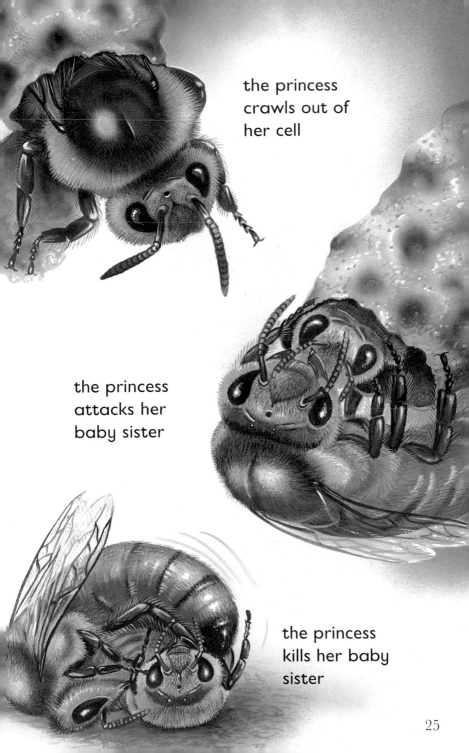

the princess
crawls out of
her cell

the princess
attacks her
baby sister

the princess
kills her baby
sister

Then she goes to see all the prince bees, or drones – the only males in the city.

She flies from the hive. All the males or drones follow. She flies higher and higher into the sky. One by one, the male bees become exhausted and die, crashing to the ground. Eventually, only a few princes are left. She mates with as many as she can and the princes die.

The new young queen returns to the city. She gathers together many workers and other bees and they set off in a huge swarm.

She will start a new city of bees.

Bees, bumble-bees and wasps

Wasps and bumble-bees are
not the same as bees.

Bees

◆ Bees have long narrow
bodies that are usually
very dark grey – almost
black. Sometimes you can
see slightly lighter coloured
stripes going across.

◆ Bees remain awake during the winter.
They stay mostly in the hive.

◆ Bees can only get food from flowers. In winter
they live off the honey they've stored.

◆ A bee's sting has an extra jagged part. When
a bee attacks, the sting stays in its enemy.
Part of the bee's body is then ripped off and
so the bee dies.

Bumble-bees

◆ Bumble-bees are almost always much fatter-
looking and bigger than either bees or wasps.
They are a similar colour to bees but fluffier.

◆ Queen bumble-bees hibernate. All the worker
bumble-bees die in winter. Bumble-bees live
mostly in the ground in old mouse holes.

◆ They get food from flowers too, but need much more nectar than  a bee just to live.

◆ Bumble-bees hardly ever sting. But like wasps, they can sting many times.

Wasps

◆ Most wasps are yellow with black stripes. They are about the same size as bees.

◆ Queen wasps hibernate and the worker wasps all die. They make their own homes. They hang their nests in a sheltered place, often near humans because they feed on the remains of our meals.

◆ Wasps get food from flowers but can manage with other food too. They can find sugar in much of the food we throw away. That is why they can be such a nuisance on the beach or near litter bins.

◆ Wasps can sting many times. Their sting is straight so they can pull it back out.

▶ Glossary

 cell A cell is a box with six sides. It is made of wax, and used to keep honey in or as cots for baby bees.

12, 14, 19, 22, 23, 24

 comb A comb is a block of many cells.   **12, 18, 19**

 drone A male bee is called a drone.   **7, 26**

 hibernate When a bee or other animal sleeps for the winter months, we say it hibernates.   **28, 29**

 honey Honey is a sweet and stiff liquid which bees make for food.   **7, 14, 15, 28**

nectar Nectar is a sweet liquid made by flowers to help bring insects to them. **14, 15, 16, 17, 29**

 pollen Pollen is a dusty powder which flowers make to help them grow seeds. **8, 14, 15**

 swarm A swarm of bees is a large group of worker bees, and a queen bee looking for a new home. **27**

 wax Bees make a sticky yellow glue and use it to make cells and combs. This glue is called wax. It sets like plastic.

12, 18, 19, 22, 24

OXFORD

WILD READS

WILD READS will help your child develop a love of reading and a lasting curiosity about our world. See the websites and places to visit below to learn more about bees.

Bees

WEBSITES

Honey bees are at risk and need your help.
Visit these websites below to find out why bees are so important to us.

http://www.britishbee.org.uk/bees4kids/

http://www.nhm.ac.uk/kids-only/naturecams/beecam/

http://www.bumblebee.org/

PLACES TO VISIT

Bees are all around us. You will find them in lots of outdoor spaces especially where there are flowers.